Maurice Ravel

Rapsodie Espagnole
Mother Goose Suite
&
Pavane for a Dead Princess
in Full Score

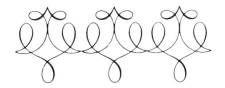

DOVER PUBLICATIONS, INC.
Mineola, New York

Bibliographical Note

This Dover edition, first published in 2001, is a new compilation of three works originally published separately. Durand et Cie, Paris, originally published *Rapsodie Espagnole* (1908) and *Ma mère l'Oye: Cinq Pièces Enfantines* (1912). *Pavane pour une infante défunte* was originally published by E. Demets, Paris (1910).
Lists of contents and instrumentation, as well as the glossary of French terms in the scores, are newly added.

International Standard Book Number: 0-486-41899-5

Manufactured in the United States of America
Dover Publications, Inc., 31 East 2nd Street, Mineola, N.Y. 11501

CONTENTS

GLOSSARY OF FRENCH TERMS
IN THE SCORES

à, with, *à 2*, both instruments
accord, tuning, *en accord*, simultaneously
animé, animez, animato
archet, bow
assez, fairly
augmentez, crescendo
au M^t, au Mouv^t, tempo primo
aussi . . . que, as . . . as
avec, with
baguettes, mallets, *baguettes d'éponge*,
    sponge mallets
beaucoup, considerably, very much
bien, very
bouché(s), stopped
calme, calm
cédez, ritardando
changez en, retune to
cordes, strings
de, of
début, beginning
(en) dehors, prominently
div. à 3, divisi in 3
dos, back
du, of the
(en) élargissant, broadening
encore, still
et, and
étouffez, damp
expressif, expressively
Fa, F
fin, end
glissez, slide
grave, solemn
jeu ordinaire, ordinario
jusqu'à, jusqu'au, up to, until
l', la, le, les, the
La, A
laissez vibrer, let ring
large, broadly, largo
las, languid
lent, lento, slow
libre de mesure, rhythmically free
mailloche, bass-drum beater
même, same
mettez, attach (mute)
Mi, E

modéré, moderato
moins, less
(l^er) Mouv^t, tempo (primo)
ôtez, remove
pas, not
(à) peine, slightly
(en se) perdant, dying away
petite, small
(un) peu, (a) little, *peu à peu*, gradually
plus, more, *de plus en plus*, more and more
prenez, take, change to
presque, almost
que, than
ralenti, ralentir, ralentissez, rallentando
rapide, quickly
Ré, D
(en) Récit, recitative(like)
reprenez, resume with
(en) retenant, meno mosso
retenez, retenu, meno mosso
rythme, rhythm
sans, without
Si, B
Sol, G
son(s) naturel(s), ordinario
sons réels, sounding pitches
sourdine(s), mute(s)
soutenu, sustained
subitement, suddenly
suivez, follow, colla (parte)
sur, on
temps, beat
touche, fingerboard
toujours, always, remain
toutes, all
très, very
trop, too
un, une, a
unis, unisono
Ut, C
valse, waltz
vif, vivace, lively
1., 1°, 1re, 2., 2°, 2de, 3., 3°, 3me, first,
    second, third
4^eC., 4th string

Rapsodie Espagnole
Mother Goose Suite
&
Pavane for a Dead Princess
in Full Score

RAPSODIE ESPAGNOLE
INSTRUMENTATION

2 Piccolos [Petites Flûtes, p^{tes} Fl.]
2 Flutes [Grandes Flûtes, G^{des} Fl.]
2 Oboes [Hautbois, H^{tb}]
English Horn [Cor Anglais, Cor A.]
2 Clarinets (B♭) [Clarinettes en Si♭, Cl.]
Bass Clarinet (B♭) [Clarinette basse en Si♭, Cl.B.]
3 Bassoons [Bassons, B^{ons}]

Sarrusophone [Sarr.]
4 Horns [Cors chromatiques en Fa, Cors]
3 Trumpets [Trompettes, Tromp.]
3 Trombones [Tromb.]
Tuba

4 Timpani [Timbales chromatiques, Timb.]
Bass Drum [Grosse-Caisse, Gr.C.]
Cymbals [Cymbales, Cymb.]
Triangle [Trg.]
Tambourine [Tambour de Basque, T. de B.]
Castanets [Castagnettes, Cast.]
Military Drum [Tambour Militaire, Tamb.]
Tam-tam [T.-T.]
Xylophone
Celesta

2 Harps [Harpes]

Violins I, II [Violons, V^{ons}]
Violas [Altos, Alt.]
Cellos [Violoncelles, V^{elles}]
Basses [Contrebasses, C.B.]

The Xylophone is notated at concert pitch.

The Celesta is notated an octave below concert pitch:

Tambourine ⎰ = shake the instrument.
          ⎱ = rub with the thumb.

RAPSODIE ESPAGNOLE

▶▶▶▶◀◀◀◀

I. — Prélude à la nuit

II.— Malagueña

III.— Habanera

(1895)

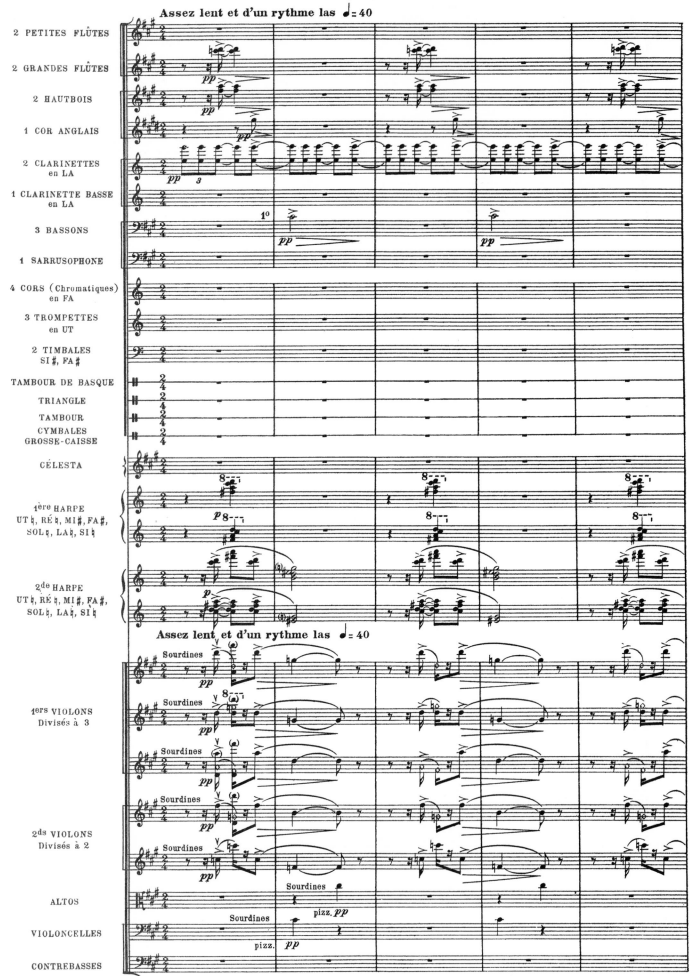

9
Ptes Fl.
Gdes Fl.
Htb
Cor A.
Cl.
Cl. B.
Bons
Cors
Tromp.
1º 2º
Sourdines
T. de B.
Trg.
Cymb.
1re Harpe
Ré ♯
Ré ♮
Ut ♯
Fa ♮
Sol ♮
2de Harpe
gliss.
Si ♮
Ré ♭, Sol ♭
Vons
Div. arco
sur le La
port.
Unis. +
Div.
pizz.
arco
Unis.
Alt.
Div. à 2
pizz
velles
C. B.
Unis.
Div.

IV.— Feria

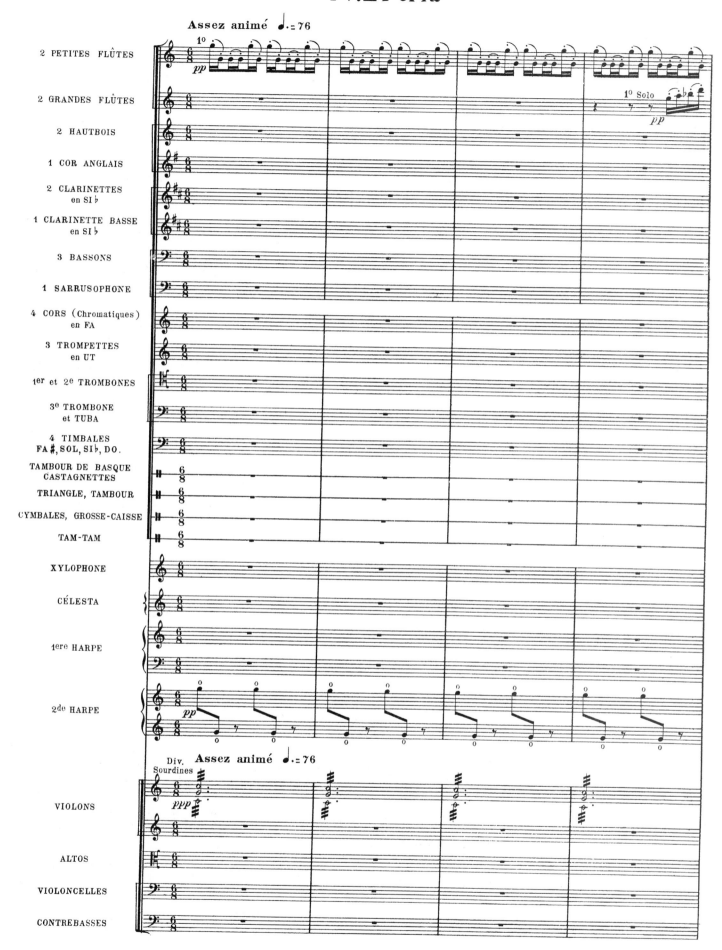

(★) Glissez en effleurant la corde *du côté du chevalet*
Slide the finger lightly over the string near the bridge.

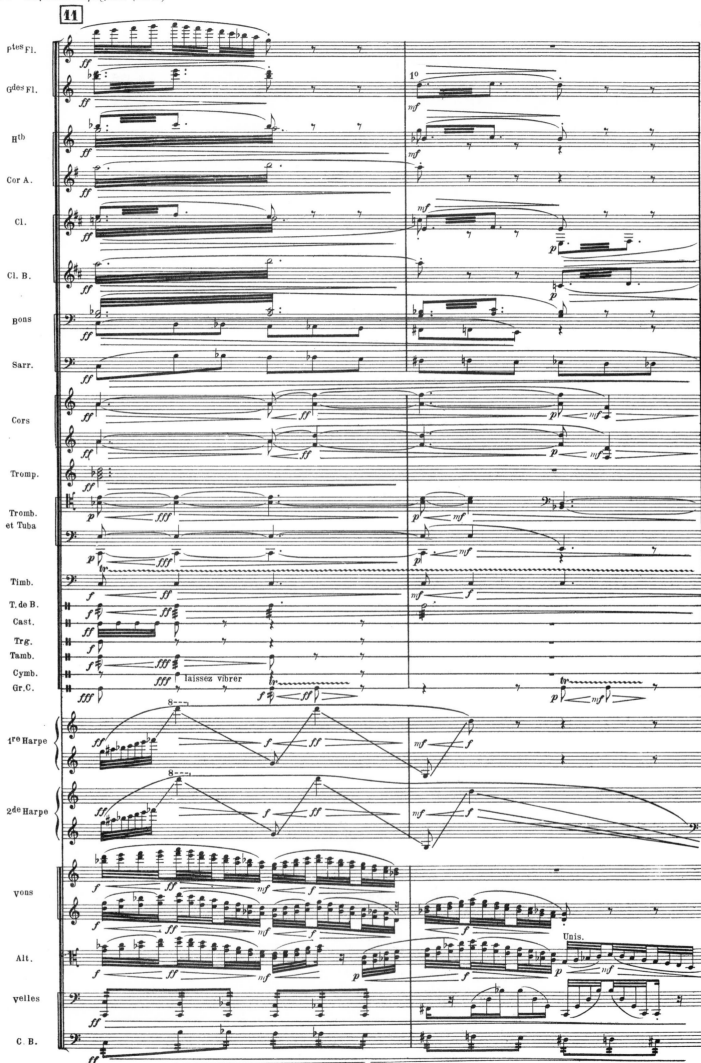

Ptes Fl.
Gdes Fl.
Htb
Cl.
Bons
Cors
Sourd.
Célesta
1re Harpe
1 1er von Solo
1ers vons Div. à 4
ôtez les Sourdines
2ds vons
1 Alt. Solo
Alt.
ôtez les Sourdines
4 velles Soli
gliss.
1 velle Solo
Sourdines
velles
Sourdines
C. B.
ôtez les Sourdines

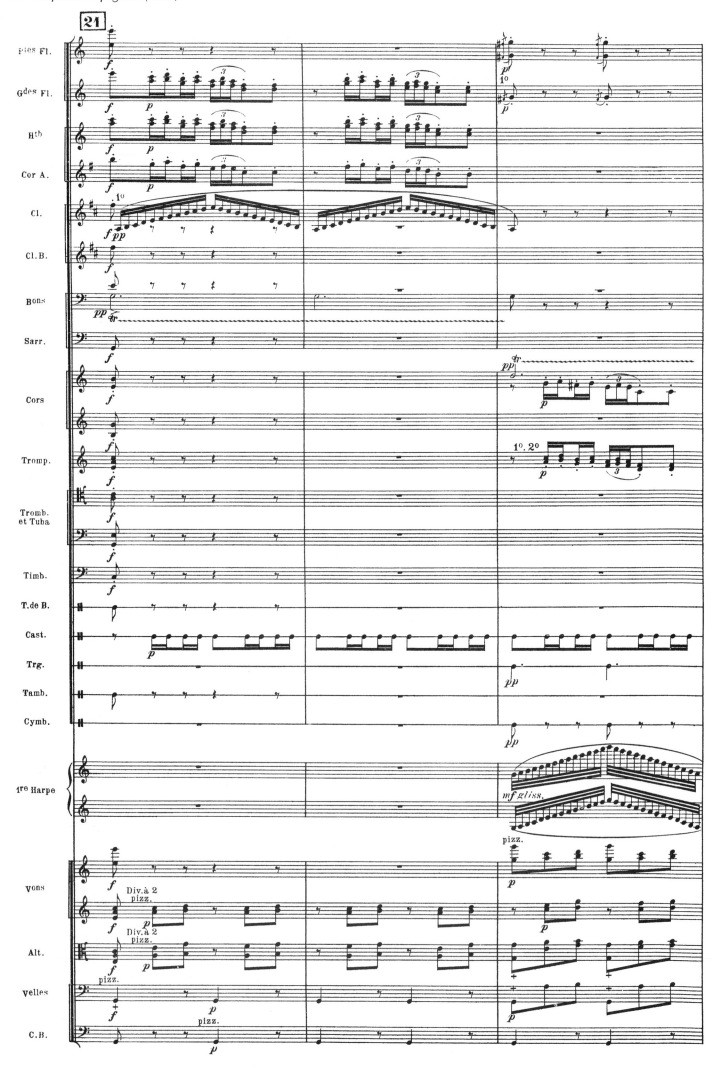

26
Un peu retenu
ptes Fl.
Gdes Fl.
Htb
Cor A.
Cl.
Cl. B.
Bons
Sarr.
Cors
Tromp.
Tromb. et Tuba
Timb.
T. de B.
Cast.
Tamb.
Cymb.
Gr. C.
Harpes
Vons
Alt.
Velles
C. B.
à 2
laissez vibrer
gliss.
Un peu retenu

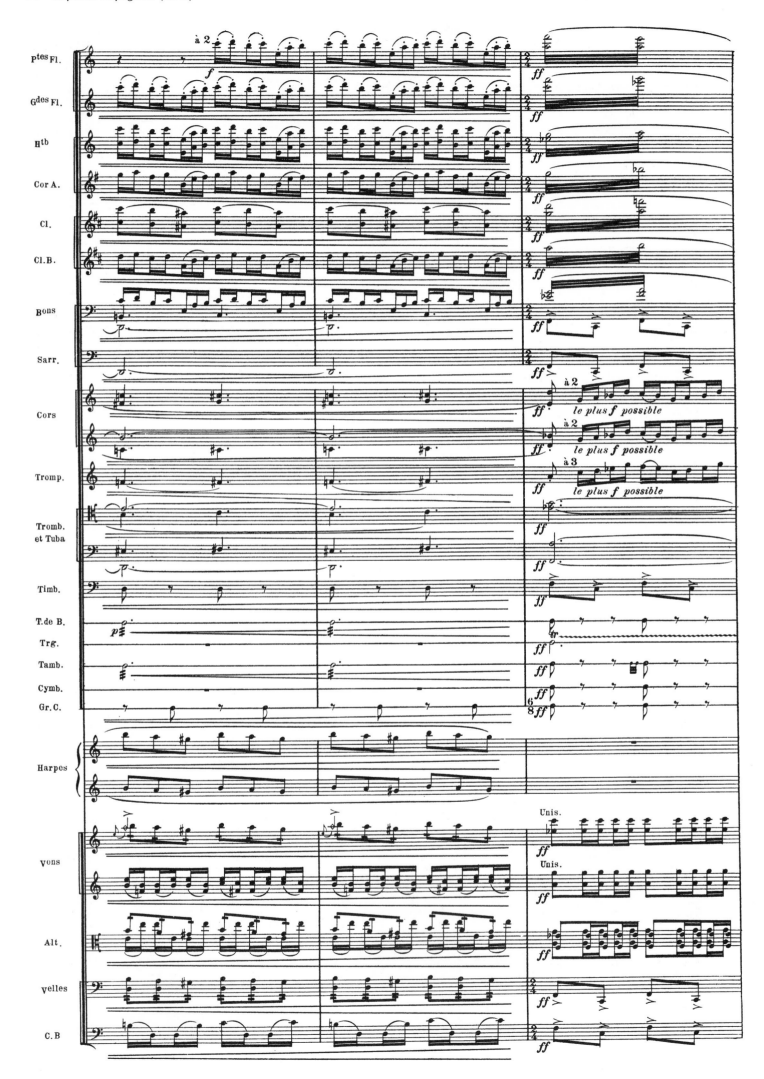

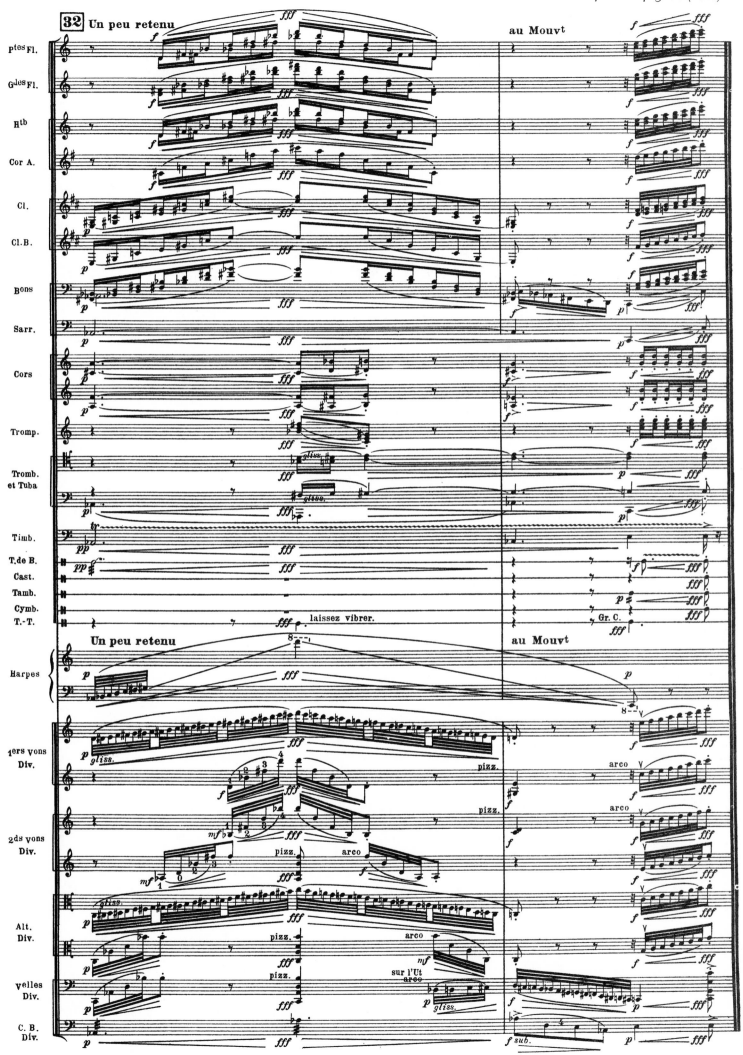

MOTHER GOOSE SUITE
INSTRUMENTATION

2 Flutes [Grandes Flûtes, G^{des} Fl.] (one Fl. = Piccolo)
2 Oboes [Hautbois, H^{tb}] (one Ob. = English Horn)
2 Clarinets (B♭, A) [Clarinettes en Si♭, La; Cl.]
2 Bassoons [Bassons, B^{ons}] (2nd Bsn. = Contrabassoon [Contrebasson, C.B^{on}])

2 Horns (F) [Cors chromatiques en Fa, Cors]

Timpani [Timbales, Timb.]
Triangle [Trg.]
Cymbals [Cymbales, Cymb.]
Bass Drum [Grosse-Caisse, Gr.C.]
Tam-tam [T.T.]
Xylophone [Xylo.]
Glockenspiel with Keyboard [Jeu de Timbres à Clavier, j. de T.]
Celesta

Harp [Harpe]

Violins I, II [Violons, V^{ons}]
Violas [Altos, Alt.]
Cellos [Violoncelles, V^{elles}]
Basses [Contrebasses, C.B.]

MA MÈRE L'OYE

5 PIÈCES ENFANTINES

❧❧❧❧❧❧❧❧❧

I.– Pavane de la Belle au bois dormant.

II.- Petit Poucet

Il croyait trouver aisément son chemin par le moyen de son pain qu'il avait semé
partout où il avait passé; mais il fut bien surpris lorsqu'il n'en put retrouver une
seule miette; les oiseaux étaient venus qui avaient tout mangé. (Ch. Perrault.) *

*He thought he would be able to find the path easily by means of the bread he had strewn wherever he had walked. But he was quite surprised when he was unable to find a single crumb; the birds had come and eaten them all. (Charles Perrault)

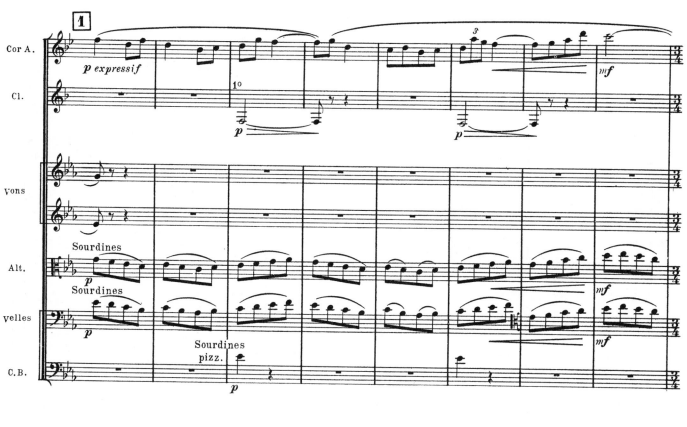

III.– Laideronnette, Impératrice des Pagodes.

*Elle se déshabilla et se mit dans le bain. Aussitôt pagodes et pagodines se mirent à chanter et à jouer des instruments: tels avaient des théorbes faits d'une coquille de noix; tels avaient des violes faites d'une coquille d'amande; car il fallait bien proportionner les instruments à leur taille. (Mme d'Aulnoy: Serpentin Vert) ***

(*) *Le Ré♯ grave étant obligé, les contrebasses à 4 cordes devront baisser le Mi d'un demi-ton.*

Since low D♯ is called for, four-string double basses must lower their E-strings a semitone.

*She undressed and got into the bath. Immediately the toy mandarins and mandarinesses began to sing and to play instruments. Some had theorbos made from walnut shells; some had viols made from almond shells; for the instruments had to be of a size appropriate to their own. (Mme d'Aulnoy, *Serpentin Vert*)

IV.– Les entretiens de la Belle et de la Bête

–«Quand je pense à votre bon cœur, vous ne me paraissez pas si laid.»–«Oh! dame oui! j'ai le cœur bon, mais je suis un monstre»–«Il y a bien des hommes qui sont plus monstres que vous.»–«Si j'avais de l'esprit, je vous ferais un grand compliment pour vous remercier, mais je ne suis qu'une bête.

...La Belle, voulez-vous être ma femme?»–«Non, la Bête!...»

–«Je meurs content puisque j'ai le plaisir de vous revoir encore une fois.»–«Non, ma chère Bête, vous ne mourrez pas: vous vivrez pour devenir mon époux!»... La Bête avait disparu et elle ne vit plus à ses pieds qu'un prince plus beau que l'Amour qui la remerciait d'avoir fini son enchantement. (Mme Leprince de Beaumont) *

*"When I think of your good heart, you do not seem so ugly." "Oh, I should say so! I have a good heart, but I am a monster." "There are many men who are more monstrous than you." "If I were witty I would pay you a great compliment to thank you, but I am only a beast."

"Beauty, would you like to be my wife?" "No, Beast!"

"I die happy because I have the pleasure of seeing you once again." "No, my dear Beast, you shall not die. You shall live to become my husband." . . . The Beast had disappeared, and she beheld at her feet a prince more handsome than Amor, who was thanking her for having lifted his spell. (Mme Leprince de Beaumont)

6
1er Mouvt (Un peu plus lent)
Pte Fl.
Trg.
Harpe
p
gliss.
pp
pp
8
sans Sourdine
1er Mouvt (Un peu plus lent)
1 Von Solo
pp très expressif
Sourdines
mp
Sourdines
pp
Sourdines
pp
mp
pp
mp
mp

Ral. - - - Plus lent
Pte Fl.
pp
8
Harpe
pp
1 Von Solo
Ral. - - - Plus lent
sur le La
sur le Sol
Vons
pp
Alt.
pp
sans Sourdine
1 Velle Solo
p très expressif
Velles
pp
pp
C. B.

V._Le jardin féerique

PAVANE FOR
A DEAD PRINCESS
INSTRUMENTATION

2 Flutes
Oboe [Hautbois]
2 Clarinets (Bb) [Clarinettes en Sib]
2 Bassoons [Bassons]

2 Natural Horns (G) [Cors simples en sol]

Harp [Harpe]

Violins I, II [Violons]
Violas [Altos]
Cellos [Violoncelles]
Basses [Contre-Basses]

PAVANE POUR UNE INFANTE DÉFUNTE

pour petit orchestre